W9-BWT-820

THE TEMPERATE FOREST

DISCOVER THIS WOODED BIOME

FREDERICK COUNTY PUBLIC LIBRARIES

Philip Johansson

Enslow Elementary
an imprint of
Enslow Publishers, Inc.
40 Industrial Road
Box 398
Berkeley Heights, NJ 07922
USA

http://www.enslow.com

Enslow Elementary, an imprint of Enslow Publishers, Inc.
Enslow Elementary® is a registered trademark of Enslow Publishers, Inc.

Copyright © 2015 by Philip Johansson

Originally published as *The Temperate Forest: A Web of Life* in 2004.

All rights reserved.

No part of this book may be reproduced by any means without the written permission of the publisher.

Library of Congress Cataloging-in-Publication Data

Johansson, Philip.
    The temperate forest : discover this wooded biome / Philip Johansson.
        pages cm. — (Discover the world's biomes)
    Originally published as The temperate forest: a web of life in 2004.
    Includes bibliographical references and index.
    ISBN 978-0-7660-6415-7
    1. Forest ecology—Juvenile literature. I. Title. II. Series: Johansson, Philip. Discover the world's biomes.
    QH541.5.F6J626 2015
    577.3—dc23

                                        2014027457

Summary: "Discusses the plants and animals of the temperate forest biome, including their roles in the food chain"—
Provided by publisher.

Future editions:
Paperback ISBN: 978-0-7660-6416-4
EPUB ISBN: 978-0-7660-6417-1
Single-User PDF ISBN: 978-0-7660-6418-8
Multi-User PDF ISBN: 978-0-7660-6419-5

Printed in the United States of America

102014 Bang Printing, Brainerd, Minn.

10 9 8 7 6 5 4 3 2 1

To Our Readers: We have done our best to make sure all Internet addresses in this book were active and appropriate when we went to press. However, the author and the publisher have no control over and assume no liability for the material available on those Internet sites or on other Web sites they may link to. Any comments or suggestions can be sent by e-mail to comments@enslow.com or to the address on the back cover.

♻ Enslow Publishers, Inc., is committed to printing our books on recycled paper. The paper in every book contains 10% to 30% post-consumer waste (PCW). The cover board on the outside of each book contains 100% PCW. Our goal is to do our part to help young people and the environment, too!

Interior Photo Credits: © 1999 Artville, LLC, pp. 10–11. © Corel Corporation, pp. 24 (maple leaf, ferns, grosbeak, rabbit, fox, bobcat, woodpecker, beetle, fungi), 28 (both). Dover Publications, Inc., pp. 5, 12, 18, 25, 34. Shutterstock.com: Bernadette Heath, pp. 24 (wildflowers), 32; Bildagentur Zoonar GmbH, pp. 22, 24 (raccoon); Dave Allen Photography, p. 7; David Byron Keener, p. 23; djgis, pp. 21 (background), 30; dugdax, p. 24 (oak tree); Emi, p. 40; Erika J Mitchell, pp. 21 (cranberries), 31, 33; Erni, p. 35; Kassia Marie Ott, pp. 39, 44; Klattu, p. 16; Margaret M Stewart, p. 36; Matthew Dixon, p. 9; Mike Truchon, p. 41; ninikas, p. 27; perm, p. 38; S.R. Maglione, pp. 21 (cougar), 42; StevenRussellSmithPhotos, p. 37; Svetlana Foote, p. 1; Taiftin, pp. 14, 17, 24 (forest landscape); Tom Reichner, p. 29; vic927, p. 26. © Thinkstock: gsagi/iStock, pp. 20, 21 (deer), 24 (deer); Lynn_Bystrom/ iStock, pp. 4, 24 (bear).

Cover Credits: Lightwriter1949/iStock/© Thinkstock (fawns); owatta/Shutterstock.com (Earth illustration).

Dr. Roger Powell is a biologist from North Carolina State University. He studies the behavior and ecology of black bears in Pisgah National Forest, North Carolina, with his partner, Dr. Michael Mitchell of Auburn University. The volunteers in Chapter 1 are from Earthwatch Institute, a nonprofit organization. Earthwatch supports field science and conservation through the participation of the public. See www.earthwatch.org for more information.

CONTENTS

A black bear in the temperate forest.

Chapter 1

A Forest for Bears

Black bears live throughout many of the forests of North America. Although they are common in some areas, few people know black bears as well as Dr. Roger Powell. He is a biologist who has studied bears in the southern Appalachian Mountains of North Carolina for more than twenty years.

Powell steps lightly as he approaches a thicket of maple trees where he set a bear trap the day before. Two volunteers have followed him for miles down the steep trail, their first time to the site. The trail is soaked from last night's rain, typical for late May. The air is filled with the heavy, sweet smell of rotting leaves. Spring flowers dot the forest floor.

As Powell and the volunteers arrive at the thicket, they see a large black bear caught in the trap. He weighs about 200 pounds (90 kilograms), as much as a large man. The special leg-hold trap is designed not to injure the animal. The bear's rich black fur shines in the sunlight sifting through the trees. He stamps his front feet and huffs as he watches the team approach.

Measure for Measure

With expert care, Powell gives the trapped bear a poke with a syringe on the end of a long stick. The shot contains a drug that makes the bear drowsy and harmless for less than an hour. Within minutes, the volunteers help to release the huge animal from the trap. The bear's coat is soft and thick, and they can feel his strong muscles underneath. Then the team weighs and measures the sleeping bear. To weigh him, they sling him into a tarp and hang him from a large scale. They measure the length of the bear's limp body and his legs. One volunteer pulls the bear's lips back

The sun sets over the forests of the Great Smoky Mountains, which are part of the Appalachian Mountains, along the Tennessee-North Carolina border.

while Powell checks his teeth for wear or decay. They also look for parasites, such as ticks, living on his skin or in his ears. This information helps Powell determine the health of the bear.

Finally, Powell attaches a radio collar to the big animal, fastening it with bolts. The radio collar will allow the team to track this bear through the woods for the next two or three years. The team will be able to learn where in the forest he visits most often, and where he finds food.

Learning From Bears

Roger Powell and his volunteer assistants want to understand what parts of the forest bears choose to live in. These areas provide the food and shelter the bears need to survive. Land managers can protect these areas to help keep bears as part of the forest community.

The type of forest where Powell studies black bears is called temperate forest. It is a familiar environment to people living in the eastern United States, and it is the home of many well-known plants and animals. Biologists like Powell study plants and animals of the forest to understand how the forest community works.

WHAT IS A BIOME?

The temperate forest is one kind of biome. A biome is a large region of Earth where certain plants and animals live. They survive in the biome because they are well suited to the climate found in that area. The climate is a result of the temperatures and amounts of rainfall that usually occur during a year.

Each biome has plants that may not be found in other biomes. Trees are the main plants in forests, but they do not grow in deserts. Cacti grow in deserts, but not in the tundra. The animals that eat these plants add to the living community of a biome.

LEGEND

 Tundra

 Taiga

 Temperate forest

 Grassland

 Desert

 Rain forest

 Chaparral

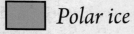 Mountain zone

Polar ice

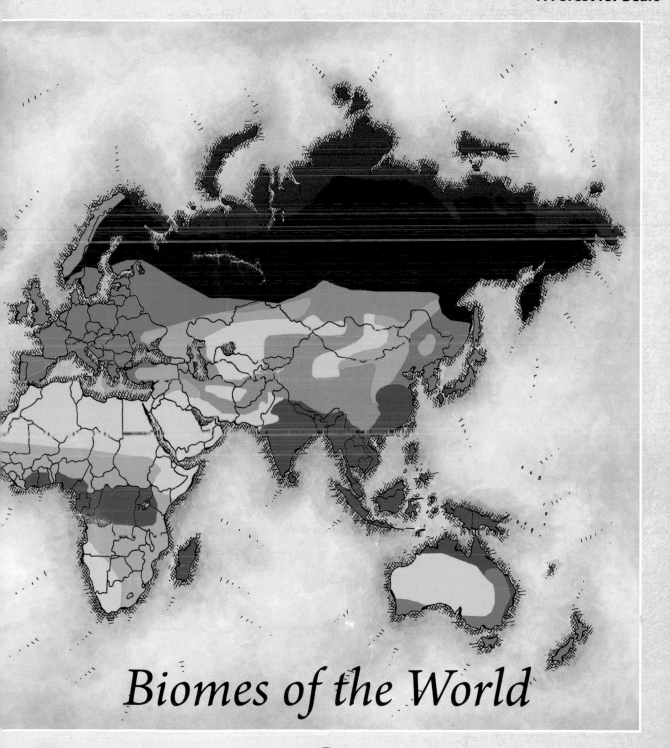

Biomes of the World

Chapter 2

The Temperate Forest Biome

Temperate forests form a strip of large, bright green areas across the northern continents of the world. There are temperate forests in North America, Europe, and Asia. These are bordered to the north by dark green boreal forests, or taiga. There are also small patches of temperate forest in the southern hemisphere, in South America, Australia, and southern Africa.

Walking through a temperate forest in summer, one is struck by the amazing variety of trees spreading their branches overhead. Each tree has its own type of bark, from light and smooth to dark and flaky. A wealth of lush green leaves whispers in the breeze, and every type of tree has its own leaf shape.

Temperate Forest Weather

Temperate forests have four distinct seasons: spring, summer, autumn, and winter. Unlike colder biomes, where winter is the longest season, the seasons in temperate areas are more equal in length. The growing season (spring, summer, and autumn) is long, up to nine months without frost. This allows plenty of time for lush green growth in the forest. During the growing season, the plants gather energy from the sun for the entire forest community.

Temperate refers to the comfortable range of temperatures throughout the year in these forests. The typical coldest temperature for winter is –20 degrees Fahrenheit (–29 degrees Celsius). Summers seldom get hotter than 95 degrees Fahrenheit (35 degrees Celsius). The average over the whole year, about 50 degrees Fahrenheit (10 degrees Celsius), is moderate.

In temperate forests, no season gets more precipitation than another. Rain or snow falls evenly throughout the year.

During the growing season, the temperate forest is filled with green leaves.

The forests get between 30 and 60 inches (75 and 150 centimeters) of precipitation each year. This is twice as much as falls in grasslands, and is second only to the amount of precipitation in tropical rain forests. In the winter, the forest faces dry conditions because almost all the water is locked up in snow and ice.

The Forest Soil

The soils of temperate forests are rich and brown. They are built up from years of falling leaves, which break down into soil. The ground is soft underfoot and often smells of rotting leaves. Underneath the e soil is well drained, allowing water to flow to the tree deep below.

Trees in temperate forests need a lot of nutrients to grow their leaves every summer. Nutrients are chemicals that plants take from the soil to help them live and grow. Each spring, the leaves that fell the previous autumn are broken down by soil life. Worms, insects, fungi, bacteria, and other life in the soil survive on the rotting leaves. They also break down fallen branches and logs. The soil life releases nutrients into the soil. These nutrients can be used again by the living trees and other plants of the forest.

The moderate range of seasons and rich soil in the temperate forests allow thick forests to grow. You will learn how the forest plants and animals are ideally suited to live in these conditions.

The rich brown soil is covered with fallen leaves. The leaves will rot and turn into soil.

TEMPERATE FOREST FACTS

Four seasons: Winter, spring, summer,

drained. It has a thick layer of rotted leaves on top. It is rich in nutrients from leaves and other decaying matter.

High precipitation: Between 30 and 60 inches (75 and 150 centimeters) of precipitation falls each year.

Long growing season: Up to nine months of frost-free weather.

17

Chapter 3

Forest Communities

Communities of plants and animals live in the temperate forest. Communities are the groups of living things found together in a place. Within a community, some plants and animals depend on others. The plants and animals interact with each other every day. Each living thing has a particular role in the community.

Energy Flow in the Forest

Plants in a community trap energy from sunlight for their food. They use the sun's energy to make sugar from carbon dioxide (a gas in the air) and water from the soil. They later use the energy in the sugars to build new leaves, stems, roots, and flowers.

Some animals, such as deer and grasshoppers, eat these plants. Animals that eat only plants are called herbivores. Herbivores get their energy from plants. O_____ carnivores, eat herbivores. Red foxes, sharp-_____ spiders are carnivores. Carnivores get their energy from eating other animals. Omnivores, such as raccoons and bears, are animals that eat both plants and animals.

Soil animals and fungi start to work when plants and animals die. They help break down the dead plants and animals. They release nutrients back into the soil. Earthworms, beetles, fungi, and microbes do this job. These animals are called decomposers.

The Food Web

The flow of energy from the sun to plants to herbivores to carnivores follows a pattern called a food web. The food web connects the plants and animals of a community, showing who eats whom.

Plants and animals pass energy through the community. At each stage of the food web, some energy is lost as the plants

Deer eat plants in the forest.
They are herbivores.

A sharp-shinned hawk eats animals, such as finches. It is a carnivore.

SOME PLANTS AND ANIMALS IN THE
TEMPERATE FOREST FOOD WEB

PLANTS	HERBIVORES	CARNIVORES
Eaten by →	Eaten by →	

PLANTS	HERBIVORES	CARNIVORES
Oaks	Gray Squirrels	Red Fox
Maples	Grosbeaks	Sharp-shinned Hawks
Birches	Porcupines	Fishers
Grasses	Deer	Coyotes
Ferns	Chipmunks	Bobcats
Mosses	Moose	Woodpeckers
Wildflowers	Cottontail Rabbits	Thrushes
Raspberries	Raccoons	Warblers
	Bears	Raccoons
		Bears

SOIL LIFE

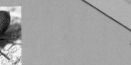

Beetles   Worms   Bacteria   Fungi

Chapter 4

Temperate Forest Plants

Temperate forests look very different in each season. The trees and other plants change with the changing temperatures and day lengths. In the winter, the ground is often covered with snow and many of the trees are bare. In the spring, leaves and tiny flowers burst from buds on the bare trees. In the summer, the trees and other plants

During the winter, the ground can be covered with snow and the branches of trees are bare.

are covered with broad leaves, filling the forest with shades of green. This is when the forest is busiest collecting energy from the sun. In autumn, many tree leaves change color and fall to the ground. This cycle repeats itself each year.

Seasons of Trees

Most trees of the temperate forest are called deciduous. This means they lose their leaves every autumn and grow them back each spring. Losing their leaves is an adaptation to help the trees survive the cold and lack of water during winter.

When the days grow shorter in the autumn, deciduous trees start to cut off the sap flowing to their leaves. The leaves lose their green color, allowing the red, yellow, or orange in them to shine through. Then the leaves fall off. The trees store sap, water, and nutrients in their roots, where they will not freeze. The trees are inactive for the winter.

When spring arrives, tree branches are covered with buds and colorful flowers.

In the spring, the deciduous trees get active again. The sap rises back up from the roots with the rising temperature. The sap brings precious water, sugars, and other nutrients to the branches. Then the trees can sprout leaves and flowers again.

Kinds of Trees

Temperate forests are made up of a few groups of deciduous trees, such as oak, hickory, maple, poplar, sycamore, birch, ash, and beech. Within each group, though, there are many species. For example, there are white oak, red oak, black oak, scarlet oak, pin oak, and willow oak. Each species has a different-shaped leaf. It is possible to tell a red maple from a silver maple by looking at the leaves.

Red maples (above) and silver maples (below) have different-shaped leaves.

Temperate forest trees have broad, flat leaves. Being broad allows the leaves to collect a lot of energy from the sun. During the growing season, these leaves collect all the energy their trees need for the whole year.

Evergreen trees are mixed with the deciduous trees, which have colorful leaves in the fall.

In some temperate forests, evergreen cone-bearing trees are mixed with deciduous trees. In northern temperate forests, evergreen spruces and firs grow. In river valleys, evergreen hemlock trees stand alongside maples and beeches. In sandy areas, evergreen pines may replace other trees.

The top branches of tall trees meet each other overhead. This forms a forest canopy.

Levels of the Forest

The tallest trees of the temperate forest grow to between 60 and 100 feet (18 and 33 meters) tall. They form a canopy in which the top branches reach out to meet each other. The dense canopy allows only some light to reach smaller trees and other plants growing beneath.

Some of these smaller trees are saplings. Saplings are young trees, waiting for a chance to grow taller. They will have a burst of growth when a nearby tree falls and leaves a hole in the canopy. Other trees just stay beneath the canopy their whole lives, catching sunlight that filters through. This area of trees growing beneath the canopy is called the understory.

Cranberries, blackberries, elderberries, and other woody plants grow beneath the saplings. These shrubs are also part of the understory. They never grow taller than a person. Herbs, ferns, and wildflowers grow even lower to the ground. Asters, buttercups, lilies, orchids, and nettles are just some of the many wildflowers that bloom here in the warm months. Mushrooms spring from the ground in the late summer, and mosses carpet damp areas.

Because they grow in different forest layers, many different types

Many shrubs, such as this highbush cranberry, grow on the forest floor. Their berries feed forest animals.

Aster is one of many wildflowers that bloom in the temperate forest.

of plants that gather energy from the sun can live together in a temperate forest. Many more species of plants live in these forests than in taiga forests to the north. The richness of plant growth in temperate forests supports the many animals in the forest food web.

PLANT FACTS

Changing with seasons: The forest changes with the different temperatures of each season, from the bare branches of winter to the many leaves of summer.

Mostly deciduous trees: Most trees lose their leaves every autumn, including maples, oaks, beeches, ashes, and birches. Some evergreen trees also grow.

Sap storage: Sap is stored in a tree's roots in autumn to avoid freezing. Sap flows back up to branches in the spring.

Broad leaves: Flat, broad leaves help deciduous trees get the maximum energy from the sun with each leaf, making the most of sunny summer months

Tree canopy lets enough sunlight through to support many other plants of various heights.

Ferns and wildflowers: Many kinds of ferns and colorful wildflowers live in the dappled light of the forest floor, bringing it to life in the growing season.

Chapter 5

Temperate Forest Animals

Using the energy and nutrients stored in temperate forest trees and other plants, a wide variety of animals thrives in this biome. Like the trees of the forest, these animals have to change their activities to deal with the changing seasons. While animals enjoy the abundance of summer in the forest, they must find a way to survive the scarcity of winter.

A shrew stays active during the winter months. It must eat half its body weight every day to survive. This shrew feasts on a worm.

Remain Active, Sleep, or Leave

Animals use three main approaches to surviving winter in temperate forests. They can remain active, become inactive, or migrate to a warmer climate.

Tracks in the snow reveal that many animals are able to remain active all winter. Some animals that do this include deer mice, shrews, rabbits, gray squirrels, gray foxes, blue jays, and white-tailed deer. Shrews have to eat half their weight in grubs, worms, and insects each day in the winter to survive. Squirrels stay warm in leaf nests. They store food through the summer and autumn to eat in the winter.

Black bears hibernate to escape the cold, but if the winter is warmer and there is food available, a black bear may leave its den.

Other animals sleep through the winter. They live off energy stored as fat in their bodies. This is called hibernation. Woodland jumping mice, bats, and groundhogs hibernate. During their long sleep, their body temperatures and heart rates drop so that they do not use their stored energy too quickly. Black bears, raccoons, and skunks rest in their dens through the winter without eating.

Most insects, such as moths, crickets, and flies, also spend the winter hidden and resting. Some crawl underground or into rotten logs for safety. Others lay their eggs in the autumn and die, leaving their eggs to survive the winter. These develop and emerge to continue their life cycles when the days grow warmer.

Finally, the other possibility is for animals to leave the temperate forest for the winter. Many birds do this, such as warblers, wrens, thrushes, tanagers, and hummingbirds. They fly to warmer areas with more food. Then they return to enjoy summer in the temperate forest, when there is plenty of food.

A luna moth becomes active when the weather warms in the spring.

Spotted salamanders live beneath the forest floor. They eat insects and other tiny animals.

Animals High and Low

In the summer, the temperate forest is alive with animals. The forest hums with the activity of insects, and birds chatter from the canopy.

Animals can be found from the forest floor up to the canopy. Many animals spend most of their time on the ground. Mice and chipmunks search the forest floor for seeds. Salamanders look for insects and other tiny animal prey on the ground. Turkeys and grouse find fallen nuts and acorns.

Other animals climb into the trees to find their food. Porcupines climb trees to find tasty leaves and twigs. Opossums find fruits and nuts in the branches. Squirrels find most of their nuts and acorns on the ground, but they run up the trees to eat in safety. Flying squirrels are especially adapted to life in the trees. They can glide from tree to tree using winglike flaps of skin between their legs.

An opossum looks for food in a tree.

A thrush enjoys a rowan berry.

Of course, the animals that make the most use of trees are birds. Some birds eat the fruits or berries and seeds found on trees. Some find insects and grubs on the trunks of trees, while others find them on the branches. Still others look for insects only on the tips of branches.

Who Eats Whom

Plant-eating animals, or herbivores, find plenty to eat in the temperate forest. Each herbivore is ideally suited to find the food it needs here. Some insects find nectar and pollen in woodland flowers, while others eat leaves. Rabbits eat grass and herbs and seeds. Deer and porcupines find leaves and buds. No matter what their diets are, though, these plant eaters get their energy from plants, which grow using the sun's energy.

A bee is covered with the pollen of a black-eyed Susan flower.

Mountain lions are one of the carnivores in the temperate forest.

Temperate forest animals divide their time between eating and watching out for carnivores that might eat them. Deer watch out for wolves and mountain lions. Birds must watch out for sharp-shinned and Cooper's hawks, which might swoop down and eat them. Even porcupines with all their quills cannot avoid being eaten. They are hunted by fishers, large members of the weasel family. Carnivores continue the forest food web.

The black bears studied by Roger Powell are important omnivores in the temperate forest. They eat both plants and animals, including grasses, berries, insects, small mammals, and dead animals. Other omnivores that live in the temperate forest include raccoons and skunks.

Temperate forest communities change through the seasons, making the most of what the forest provides. Energy flows through the plants and animals of each community to fill these forests with life.

ANIMAL FACTS

Feast or famine: Most temperate forest animals find more food in the summer than the winter, requiring special adaptations for the changing conditions.

Remaining active: Animals that remain active through the winter are constantly foraging for food to have enough energy to stay warm and survive.

Sleeping: Some animals sleep through most of the winter, living off stored fat, and emerge in the summer to continue their lives. Bears, groundhogs, frogs, and woodland jumping mice do this.

In the winter, some birds fly to warmer biomes.

Insects survive the winter: Insects wait out the cold winter as adults or in the form of eggs. They emerge to continue their life cycles in the summer.

Eating nuts: Some animals, such as turkeys and squirrels, specialize in eating the nutritious nuts and seeds that fall from trees.

Climbing trees: Many mammals have sharp claws and climb trees for food and safety. Squirrels, porcupines, raccoons, and opossums are examples of animals that climb.

WORDS TO KNOW

ADAPTATION—A trait of a plant or animal that helps it survive under the conditions of where it lives.

BIOME—An area of the earth defined by the kinds of plants that live there.

CANOPY—The top of a tree or trees, where most of the leafy branches are.

CARNIVORE—An animal that eats other animals.

CLIMATE—The average weather conditions in an area, usually measured over years. It includes temperature, precipitation, and wind speeds.

COMMUNITY—The collection of plants and animals living and interacting in an area.

DECAY—The breakdown of dead plants or animals into nutrients by bacteria, fungi, and other decomposers.

DECIDUOUS—Trees that drop their leaves in the autumn and grow new ones in the spring.

DECOMPOSERS—Soil animals and fungi that help break down dead plants and animals, releasing nutrients back into the soil.

FOOD WEB—The relationships between living things that allow the transfer of energy and nutrients from plants to herbivores to carnivores to decomposers.

HABITAT—The type of place where a certain plant or animal normally lives.

HERBIVORE—An animal that eats plants.

HIBERNATE—To spend the winter in a deep sleep, with a low body temperature and heart rate, living off stored fat.

LICHEN—A small plantlike life-form that is a mixture of both algae and fungi.

MICROBE—A very simple, very small organism made of a single cell. Some microbes help decompose dead animals and plants.

MIGRATE—To travel from one place to another on a regular schedule.

NUTRIENTS—Chemicals that plants need in order to live and grow.

OMNIVORE—An animal that eats both plants and other animals.

PARASITE—An animal that lives on or in another animal and gets its nutrients directly from its host.

PRECIPITATION—Water in the form of rain, snow, or fog.

PREDATOR—An animal that hunts other animals for food.

PREY—An animal that is hunted by another for food. Also, to kill and eat another animal.

SAPLING—A young tree.

TAIGA—A forest biome found north of the temperate forest.

TEMPERATE—Moderate, not extreme, referring to the climate of temperate forests.

UNDERSTORY—The area of small trees and shrubs growing under the tall trees of the forest.

LEARN MORE

Arnosky, Jim. *Field Trips: Bug Hunting, Animal Tracking, Bird-Watching, Shore Walking.* New York: Harper Collins, 2002.

Benoit, Peter. *Temperate Forests.* New York: Scholastic, 2011.

Crossingham, John, and Bobbie Kalman. *What Is Hibernation?* New York: Crabtree Publishing Company, 2002.

Hooper, Rosanne. *Life in the Woodlands: Animals, People, Plants.* Princeton, N.J.: Two-Can Publishers, 2000.

Johnson, Rebecca L. *A Walk in the Deciduous Forest.* Minneapolis, Minn.: Carolrhoda Books, 2000.

INDEX

APR   2016   2 1982 02896 6079